Kat's Little Black Book According to the Zodiac

Kat Cotton

© 2020 Kat Cotton

All rights reserved. Printed in the United States of America
No part of this book may be reproduced in any written,
electronic, recording, or photocopying form without
written permission of the author, Kat Cotton

Edited By: VanessaDreams, Fiverr

Cover by: Kat Cotton/ Rose Miller, Fiverr Cover Designer

ISBN: 978-1-7359616-0-6

Disclaimer: Details have been changed to protect the identities of those represented in this book. That being said, this book is my opinion of my story and how I alone remember it.

This book is dedicated to my amazing family and friends who have supported me through it all. Especially to my best friends Chris and Tina - I don't know where I would be in this life without you two. The list goes on and is extensive. I cannot say enough about the strong supportive people in my life and how lucky I am to have them.

Story Time

So, how did this happen?

It started with a title idea many years ago. I have been writing poetry ever since I can remember. This book is filled with my melancholy and bliss, leaving that bittersweet feeling heavy in the air. For many of us, such is life, filled with many mixed emotions about the string of events in our past that run deep and affect us today.

Everyday people and their experiences in love were my impetus for writing this book. My hope for sharing this story through poetry is to create connection, rather to encourage the healing that connection brings. I want to be clear these are my memories and emotions, as I alone saw them, through the lens of my experiences. These poems are not meant to be taken in abhorrent fashion or to embarrass. They are meant to look back on how much one grows emotionally over the years. This book is simply an extension of self, that hopefully will find connection with others who have ever felt the same.

Growth and positivity are not rose-colored glasses and denial. Positivity and growth are work. Positivity is how we navigate negative situations healthy fashion. For me that navigation presents itself in the form of poetry. Allowing laughter and tears to fall onto pages, landing comfortably with understanding and care, under the umbrella of healing. Though the path to healing can be long and arduous, the journey holds adventure and rediscovery.

Please enjoy the poetic tales of past loves.
Some brought bliss,
Some brought pain.
Distinguish from this what you wish.
Without further ado,
hope you find the strength I found too

Table of Contents

An Artist Lion (Leo) 15

Literary Companion (Virgo) 16

Fiery Frolic (Aries) 17

A Reply to a Leo (who once wrote me a poem) 18

Blinded (Aquarius) 19

Turbulence in the Morning (Aries) 20

Fleeting (Aquarius) 21

Serial Monogamist (Taurus) 22

Acquaintances (Cancer) 23

Nostalgia in its Finest Hour (Capricorn) 24

Perspective and All its Angles (Aquarius) 25

Chance Encounter (Aries) 26

Spatial Relationship (Leo) 27

Transitory Scoundrel (Aries) 28

Down on Duval (Aquarius) 29

Don't Bother (Cancer) 30

Self-Love (Virgo) 31

An Artist Lion
(Leo)

I always knew you'd end up here.
You were always going to be a part of my story.
Young...that's the only way to describe it.
Maybe, inexperienced.
You tried to tame me-
        It was never going to work.
I wasn't that type of woman.
Like the pencil strokes of a sketch,
you were never going to be happy with anyway.
You mattered.
In the end, only I was content.
You shattered.
For that I'm sorry.

Literary Companion
(Virgo)

Buried in books.
It's where we were happiest
most days, our best chance of escape,
outside of your bottle of course.
In each other's arms
or otherwise
Engaged.
I took you at your word,
I believed your truth.
I also believed that you would break my heart,
but rest assured you did not.
My heart, whole, but not unscathed.
My armor of emotional wounds
reads like a diary
and in it, you, the villain.
Impossible, probable but that's the narrative isn't it?
Empowering in kaleidoscope perspective,
the essence of you lingers
into the light I hoped you would walk with me.
No such luck.
Into the light without you then

Fiery Frolic
(Aries)

Chronologically, you were my second Aries.
Emotionally, you were my first
flame to gasoline.
You were the match when I simply needed light.
I like the way…
Your use of vernaculars,
physical attraction to intelligence.
Sapiosexual.
What a dalliance!
Lesson learned.
What I thought would never fade-
faded.
Sometimes that's the way of it.
Distance will do that.
In my heart, you will always carry weight.
Yet, I won't let that weigh it down.
I cared.
you cared.
                      in the end.
                           Forgiveness...
                      Friends?

A Reply to a Leo
(who once wrote me a poem)

Remember the time you wrote me a poem?

I was winded by the sentiment.

Though our ships seem to be passing in the night,

it does not undermine the importance of you.

Like music,

like laughter,

our love of Bukowski…

Like fleeting moments that live on the wings of butterflies,

time moves like hummingbirds,

swiftly.

Here we are, so far apart

that does not undermine the importance of you.

Blinded
(Aquarius)

As oil and water were never meant to mix
drawn together anyway
Always I think I knew it would end like this.
Part of my story, but not my life.
Blinded by charisma,
by youth,
by inexperience,
by the sun-
one should not stare directly at it.
Keep a distance from the heat.
Lesson learned.
Burned, 3rd degree.
Being young is not an excuse.
I never met someone so cruel and so kind
all at the same time.
Jealousy never looked good on either one of us.
Emotional safety replaced with turmoil.
Through the years you came and went.
Once, I rejected you, you didn't like that very much,
but away you were sent.
You told me it wouldn't work with him.
Jealousy never looked good on you.
I wear the scars you left on my heart like badges of pride
to show
how far I have come.
                        Progress.
Healthy goodbyes.

Turbulence in the Morning
(Aries)

Chronologically, you were my first Aries.

Emotionally, you are second fiddle.

You will never really come first.

Violent waves on the ocean-

Turbulent

Your true love was the bottle.

I would always play second to that

and third to the other women.

Unhealthy-

                    to say the least.

Emotional abuse endured,

torrid and tormenting.

I can't remember why I fell in love in the first place.

If there was something good,

I can't remember it now.

Good news

Never again

Fleeting
(Aquarius)

You were fleeting.
There is not much else to say.
Unsure you belong in the retelling of the narrative.
However brief: You were important.
Should you ever need me again, I will again be there.
Friendship...
                    Unconditional.

Serial Monogamist
(Taurus)

You were my second Taurus.
The first went speeding through like a blur in a photo.
Anecdotal at best.
So quickly that this will be the only time I mention him here-
                  And only for chronology sake.
Serial monogamist I think they call it.
We hit it off right away.
Connected like magnets.
Physical attraction.
I think you were broken before I got there.
Not sure what she did to you…
You had a sweet side-
I liked that side.
                  Brief.
Then you were gone-
                  Ghosted.
Until the day, you contacted me again.
You "remember us."
It was like winning an honorable mention-
                  Man-whore trophy.
Even then no sense in going back.
Implication of an invitation.
No thanks, goodbye.

Acquaintances
(Cancer)

19.
What did we know then?
Not much.
I always enjoyed your company.
I wanted more.
You didn't.
So, I held back.
I had better rules then.
About relationships…
About men…

What I didn't know
is that we would meet again
later in life, fleeting.
I was in no place for repeating
so, I sent you away
and acquaintances we will stay.

Nostalgia in its Finest Hour
(Capricorn)

Mere teens when we met.

I may not remember,

but I will also not forget.

The dates to dances, concerts and such.

Your friendship meant so much.

You chose her and her, over me time and time again.

So over you, I chose other men.

We never got the timing right.

Your letter said as much.

Always there, even changing my tire that night.

Through the years you came and went, but always kept in touch.

We have both moved on.

Nostalgia and memories remain.

In my heart your place is still the same.

Perspective and All its Angles
(Aquarius)

You were my third Aquarius and by far my favorite.

Your soul

Beautiful and kind.

Introductions to extensions of yourself.

Giving,

adventurous,

fearless.

I always hoped you would find her.

I knew I was not part of your life,

but an important moment in your story.

At least that is how I will author the narrative.

It's all about perspective.

No matter the view

from all angles it was important to me too.

Chance Encounter
(Aries)

Number 3, I will never learn my lesson.
I saw you today on the train platform.
It left me dizzy.
Longing for the past.
Even the times when you ignored me,
I still fought for that sliver of attention.
No doubt you will ignore me again.
Yet, you always seem to show up when it counts
Chance encounter perhaps...
But I think the universe is speaking to me in volumes I have yet to read.
My unlearned lesson coming to fruition.
Surfacing with new understanding and the ability to embrace it for what it is.
What is it?
What it is does not matter, unimportant.
Forgiveness.
Letting go.

Spatial Relationship
(Leo)

Another Leo.
You even had the same birthday as my first Leo.
I should have known better,
but like with him, I have no regrets.
You gave me space to be myself, I returned the favor.
So much distance between us, there was always plenty of space.
It didn't seem to matter in the moment as we were once close.
Even then you were professing all the reasons you chose to be alone.
Denial? Unaware?
I rebuffed the notion and wished for you, every happiness.
Dancing under the stars in the middle of the ocean.
Music.
Laughter.
Attraction.
Travel.
Distance.
It would always be the distance that would be our undoing
I see that you asked her to marry you.
Still wishing you every happiness.
No longer friends...
A small piece of me is sad for that.
Still wishing you every happiness.
Not broken,
                just moving forward.
Boundaries respected.
Parting on the best of terms.

Transitory Scoundrel
(Aries)

Like a scoundrel taking refuge,
you were never going to stay.
Denial.
Depravity.
Nonsense.
By the time I came to my senses,
you were gone
                        Blink.
                      Fleeting.
                Transitory.
It never really mattered anyway.
You were a lesson, not a path.

Down on Duval
(Aquarius)

Spring Break

Key West.

Duval Street.

You made the pedal taxi stop to get my attention-
                          Momentary

Not sure where you were going,

only of your invitation to come with.

Declined.

A shared kiss

in the street.

In the quiet of the night,

whisked away by the pedal taxi that seemed to have wings.

And away you flew

Don't Bother
(Cancer)

You were never really mine to begin with.
I'm not into your games so, I won't play.
When you think you want to say hi,
don't bother.
When you think you miss me,
think again.
I'm still picking up the broken shards,
held together with emotional duct tape and glue.
Don't worry, I will put it back together myself.
When you think you want to say hi,
don't bother.
When you think you miss me,
think again.
Boundaries and broken hearts that lay between the sheets.
Mistaken for a show of fidelity.
When you think you want to say hi,
don't bother.
When you think you miss me,
think again.
Feel free to stay away.
And should you stray near,
I will happily change course.
When you think you want to say hi,
don't bother.
When you think you miss me,
think again.

Self-Love
(Virgo)

I had this feeling I wanted to hold onto.
Ephemeral
moving
Anything but still
growth, heart ache, paired.
Fresh faced,
wearing melancholy on my sleeve.
Obscene
posturing.
Path to healing...
Pain and pandemonium ignited in the face of strength.
Not turning away from the sun or the moon.
Standing in the light,
catching fire in ways I never knew I could.

Made in the USA
Monee, IL
22 November 2020